LIFE AFTER 50

A SURVIVAL GUIDE
FOR WOMEN

By Martin Baxendale

LIFE AFTER 50 - A SURVIVAL GUIDE FOR WOMEN

Published by Silent But Deadly Publications,
21 Bisley Road, Stroud, Glos. GL5 1HF,
England.

ISBN: 0 9550500 2 2

Printed in Great Britain by spacolour.com

INTRODUCTION

The first signs of old age can creep up on you at any time. Don't let it catch you napping!

With the help of this invaluable collection of useful tips and hints, the prospect of advancing age will quickly lose its irrational fears and worries.

Instead, you will find yourself positively <u>looking forward</u> to many happy years of decrepit wrinklyness, and the chance to put these pages of helpful advice into practice.

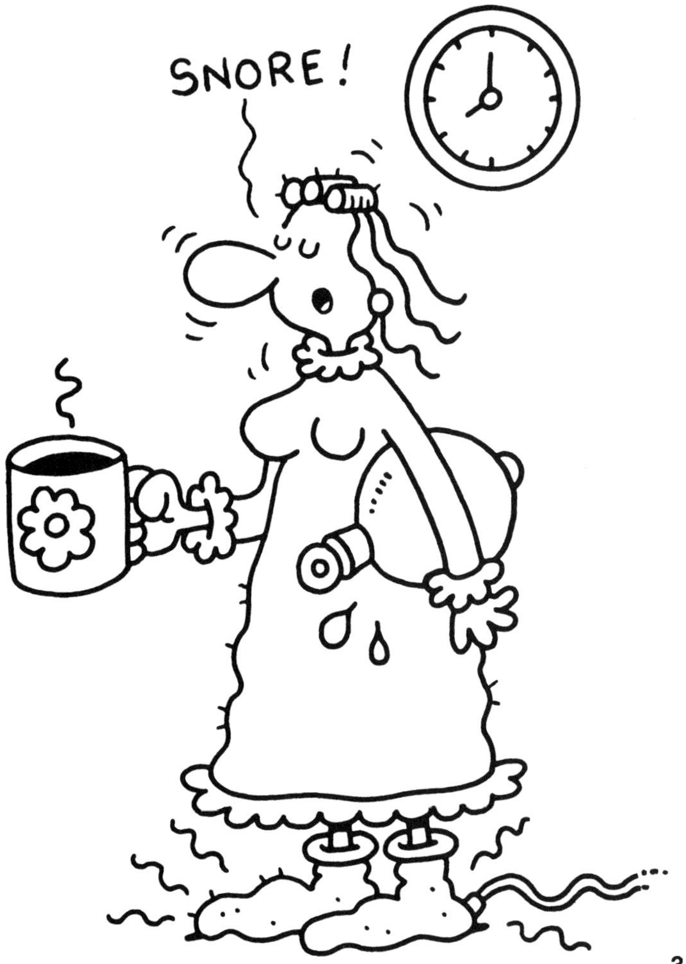
SNORE!

For example, when you get into your 50s you may find that some of your sexual preferences change a bit.

Perhaps you'll discover that you much prefer a nice comfy bed rather than the more exciting and naughty sex of your younger days, like doing it <u>outdoors</u> ....

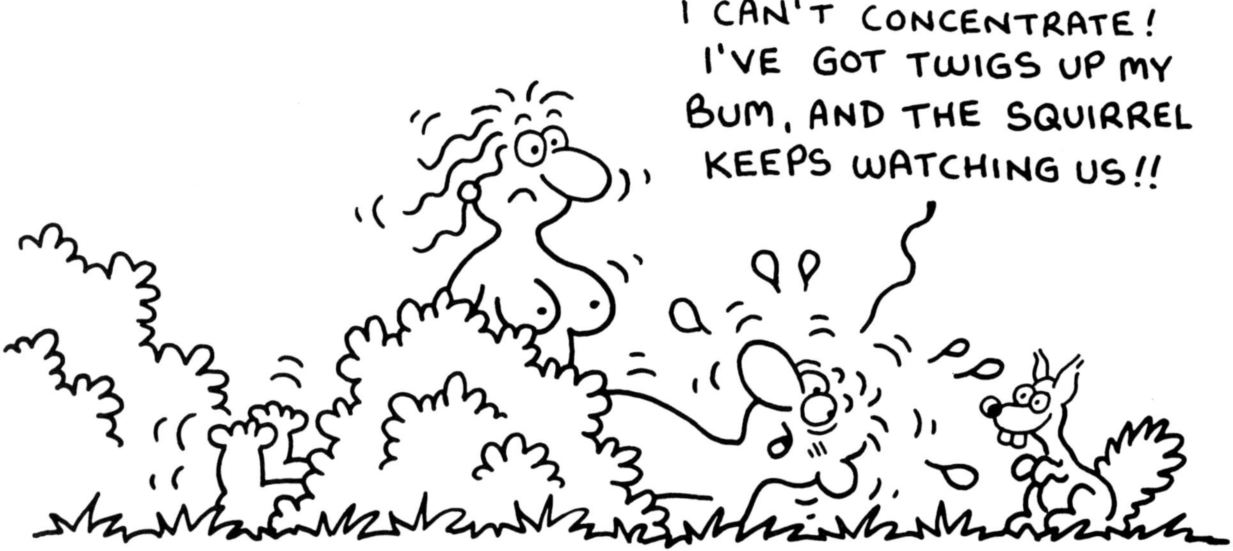
I CAN'T CONCENTRATE! I'VE GOT TWIGS UP MY BUM, AND THE SQUIRREL KEEPS WATCHING US!!

....but you can still read about that sort of wild, steamy sex while you enjoy a nice cup of hot cocoa or warm milk before a comfortable bonk in your warm, soft bed with the electric blanket on....

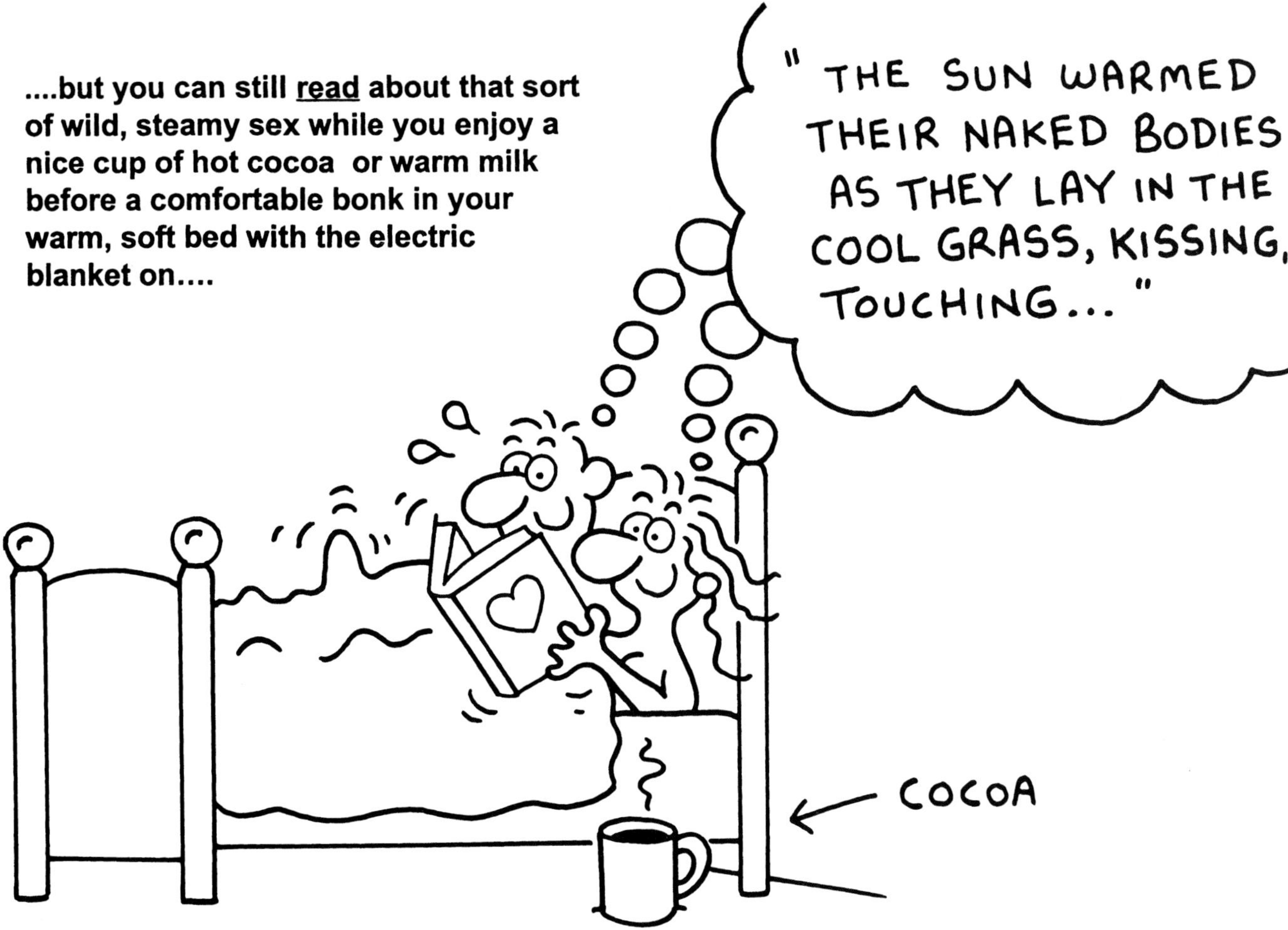

" THE SUN WARMED THEIR NAKED BODIES AS THEY LAY IN THE COOL GRASS, KISSING, TOUCHING... "
COCOA

HOW TO STAY AWAKE DURING SEX

HANDY HINT No. 1

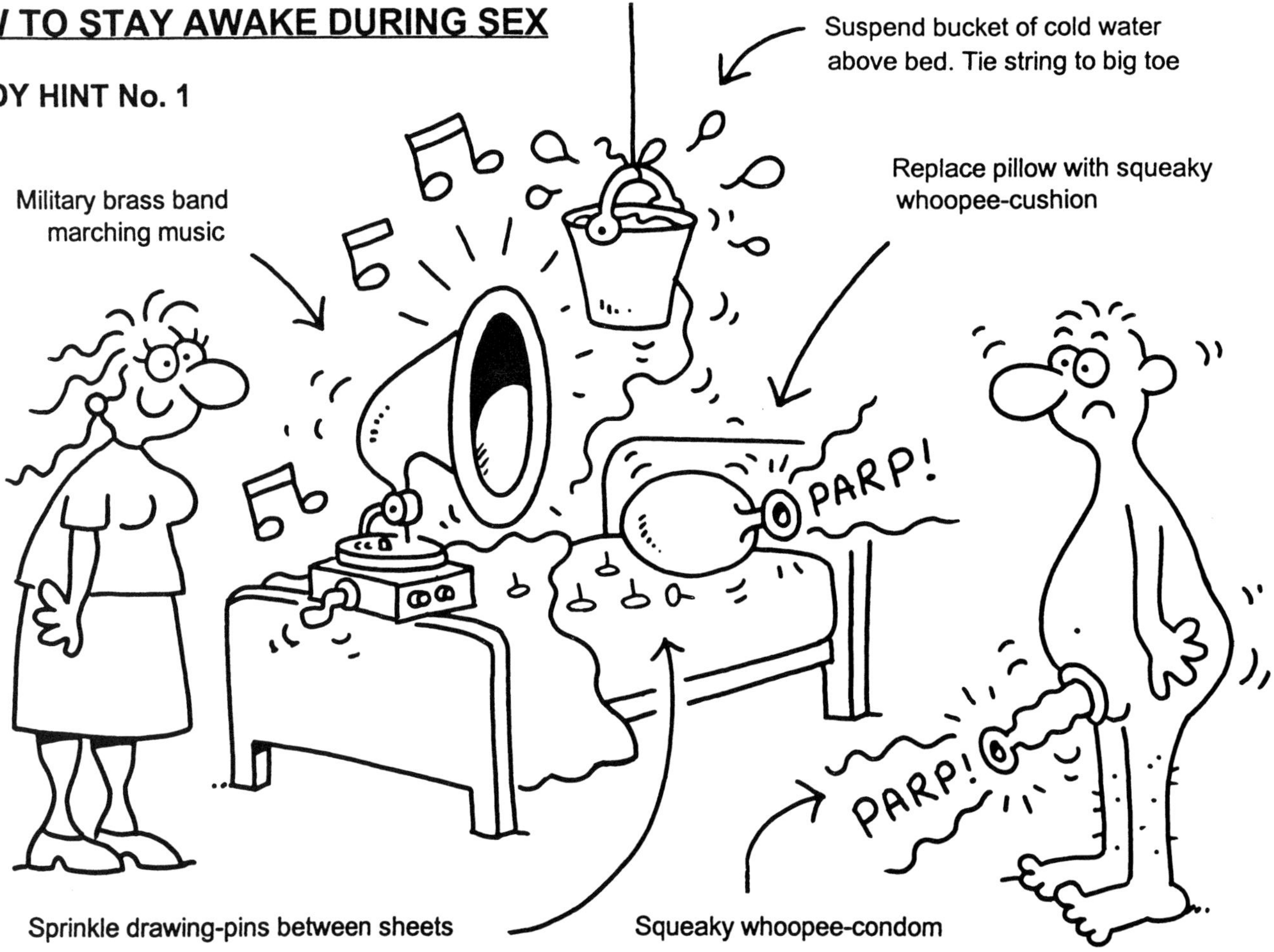

Military brass band marching music
Suspend bucket of cold water above bed. Tie string to big toe
Replace pillow with squeaky whoopee-cushion
PARP!
PARP!
Sprinkle drawing-pins between sheets
Squeaky whoopee-condom

HOW TO STAY AWAKE DURING SEX

HANDY HINT No. 2

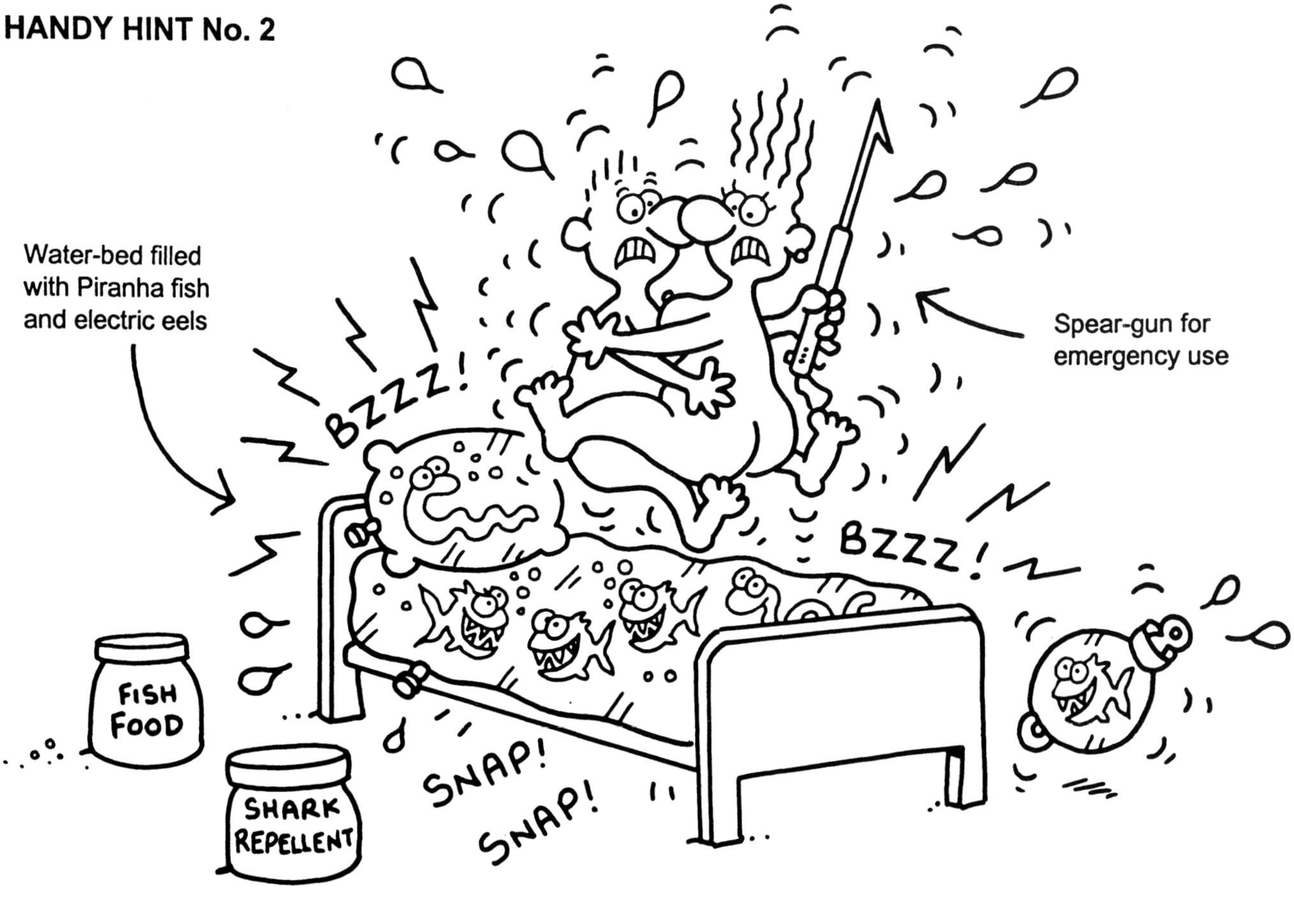

Water-bed filled with Piranha fish and electric eels
Spear-gun for emergency use
BZZZ!
BZZZ!
FISH FOOD
SHARK REPELLENT
SNAP!
SNAP!

HOW TO STAY AWAKE DURING SEX

HANDY HINT NO. 3

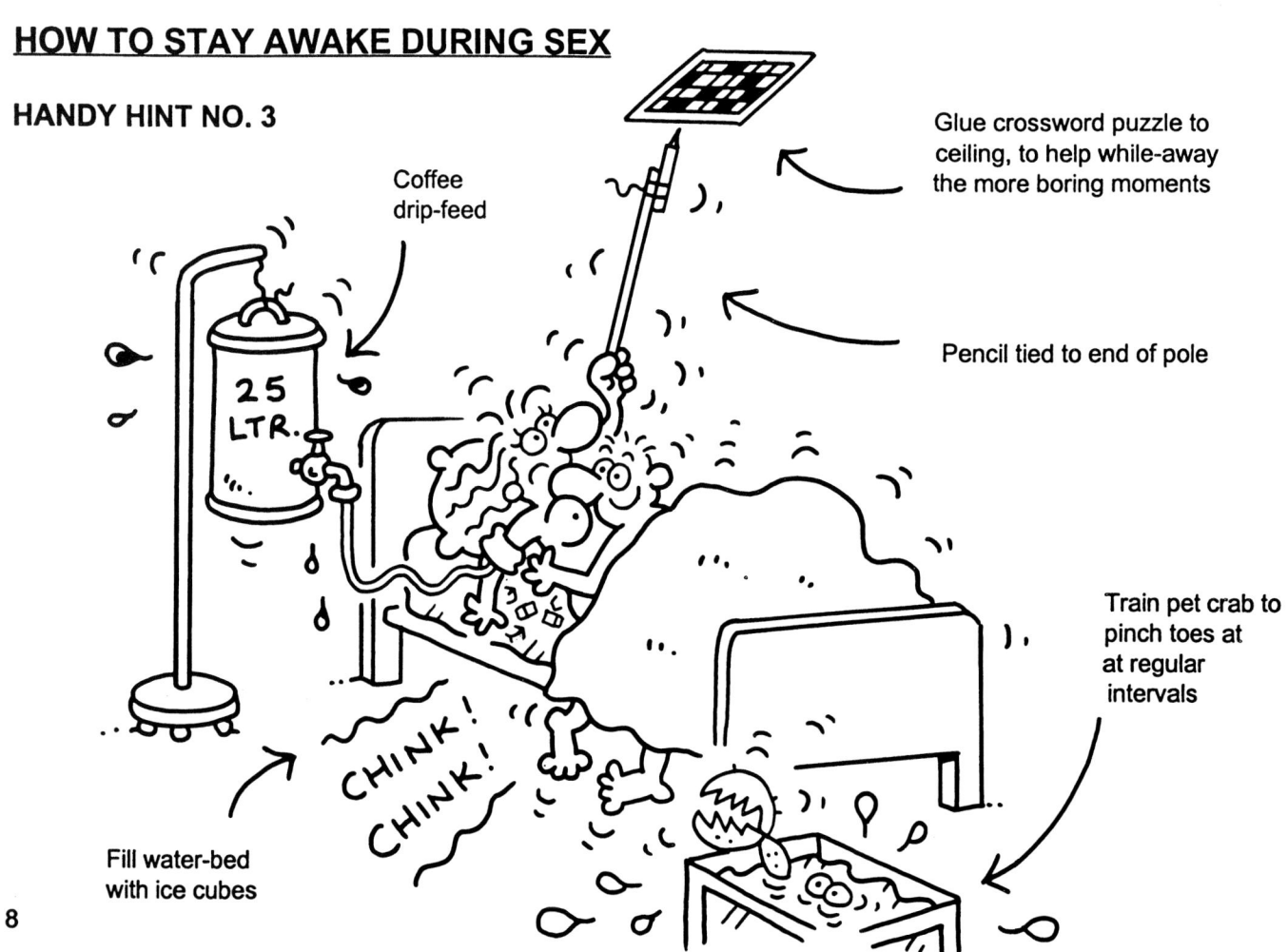

Glue crossword puzzle to ceiling, to help while-away the more boring moments

Pencil tied to end of pole

Coffee drip-feed

Train pet crab to pinch toes at at regular intervals

Fill water-bed with ice cubes

HOW TO STAY AWAKE DURING SEX

HANDY HINT No. 4

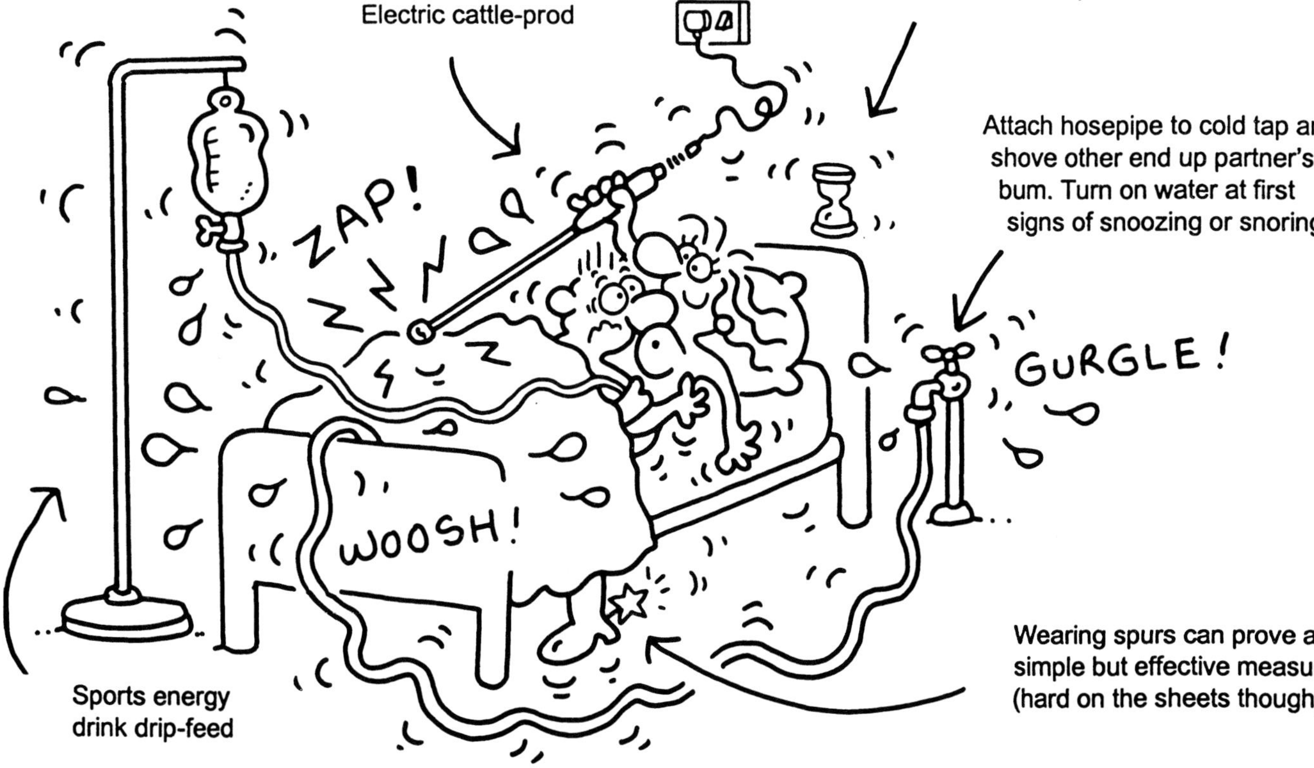
ZAP!
ZZZ
WOOSH!
GURGLE!

Egg-timer on headboard may shame aging male partner into a slightly more prolonged performance (but don't bank on it!)

Electric cattle-prod

Attach hosepipe to cold tap and shove other end up partner's bum. Turn on water at first signs of snoozing or snoring

Wearing spurs can prove a simple but effective measure (hard on the sheets though)

Sports energy drink drip-feed

AVOIDING GREY HAIRS

Essential equipment for dealing with grey hairs:

Angled wing-mirrors for spotting grey hairs

Mirror for spotting grey nose hairs

High-pressure portable shower unit

Expanding tweezers for plucking grey hairs

100 litres hair dye in pressurized tank

Mirror for spotting grey pubic hairs

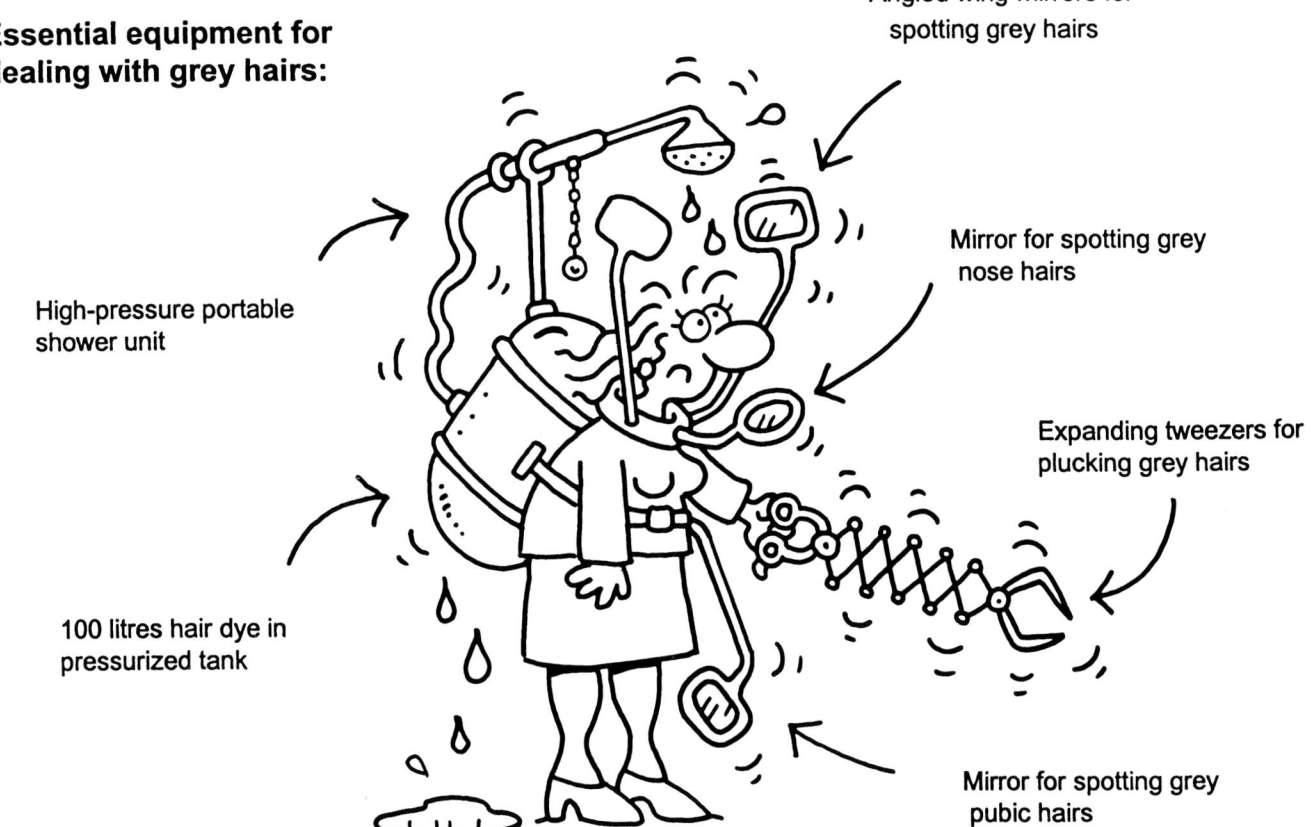

AVOIDING WRINKLES

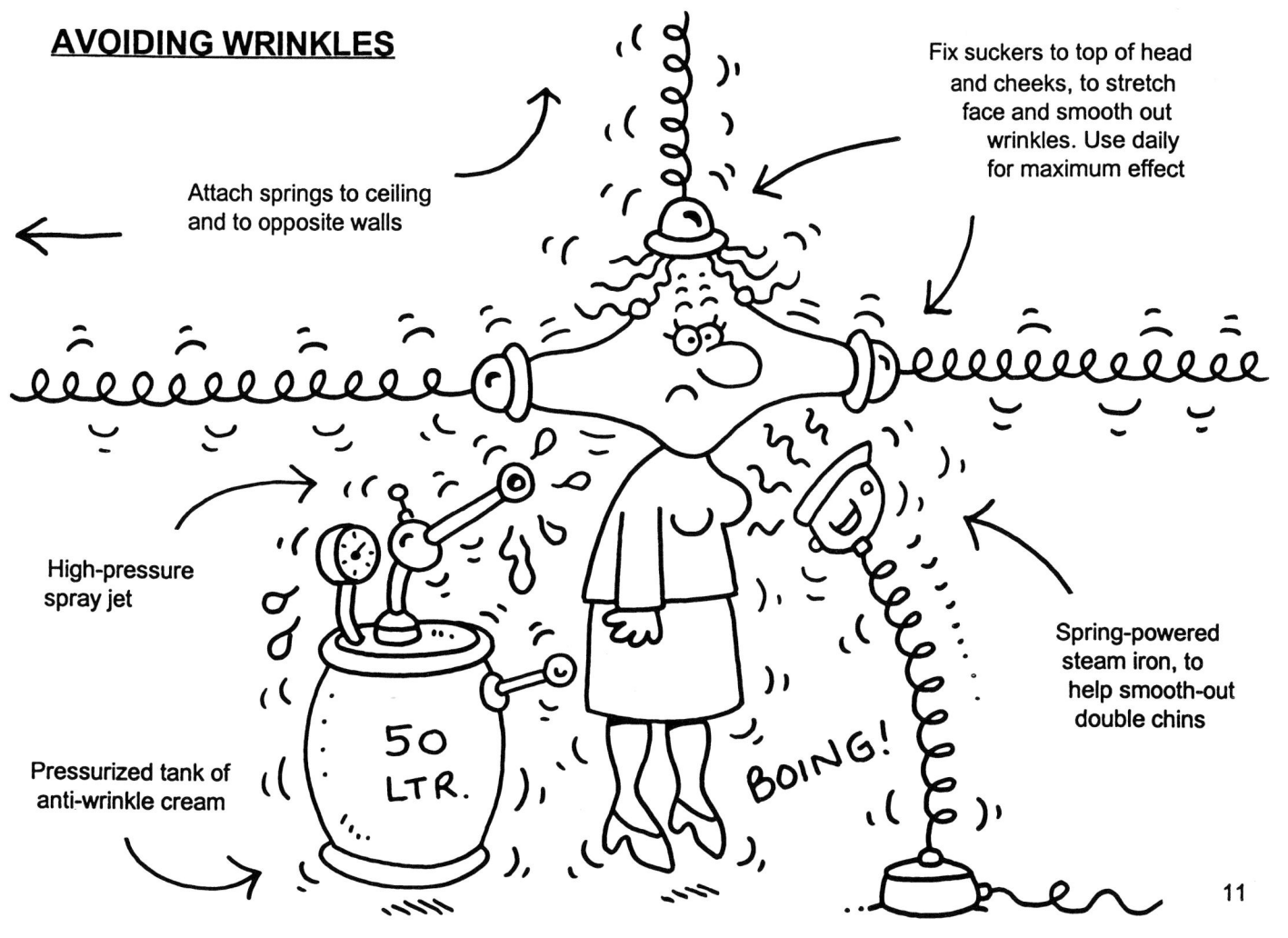

Attach springs to ceiling and to opposite walls

Fix suckers to top of head and cheeks, to stretch face and smooth out wrinkles. Use daily for maximum effect

High-pressure spray jet

Spring-powered steam iron, to help smooth-out double chins

Pressurized tank of anti-wrinkle cream

50 LTR.

BOING!

SEX WITHOUT HEART-ATTACKS

HANDY HINT No. 1

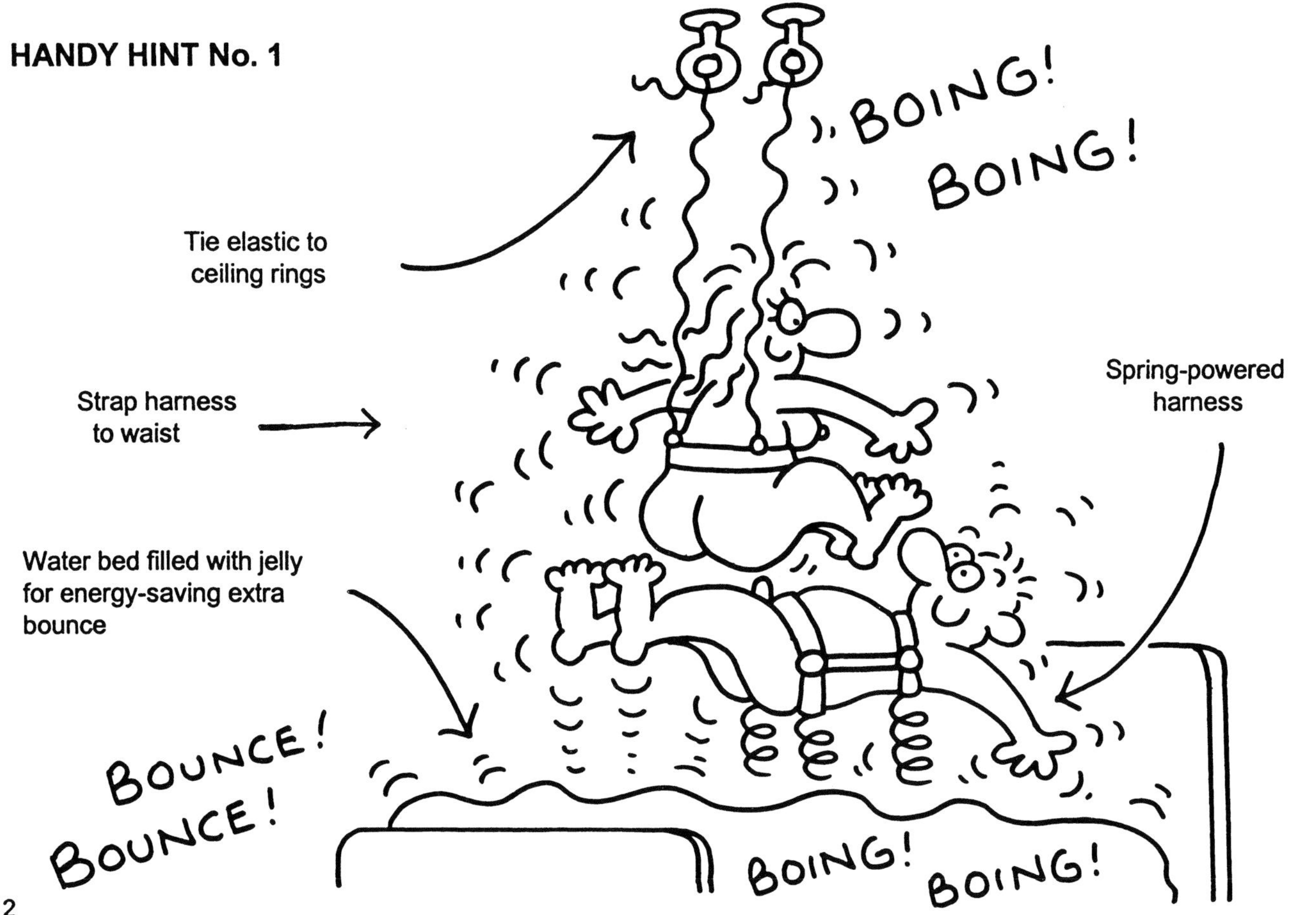
Tie elastic to ceiling rings
Strap harness to waist
Water bed filled with jelly for energy-saving extra bounce
Spring-powered harness
BOING!
BOING!
BOUNCE!
BOUNCE!
BOING!
BOING!

SEX WITHOUT HEART-ATTACKS

HANDY HINT No. 2

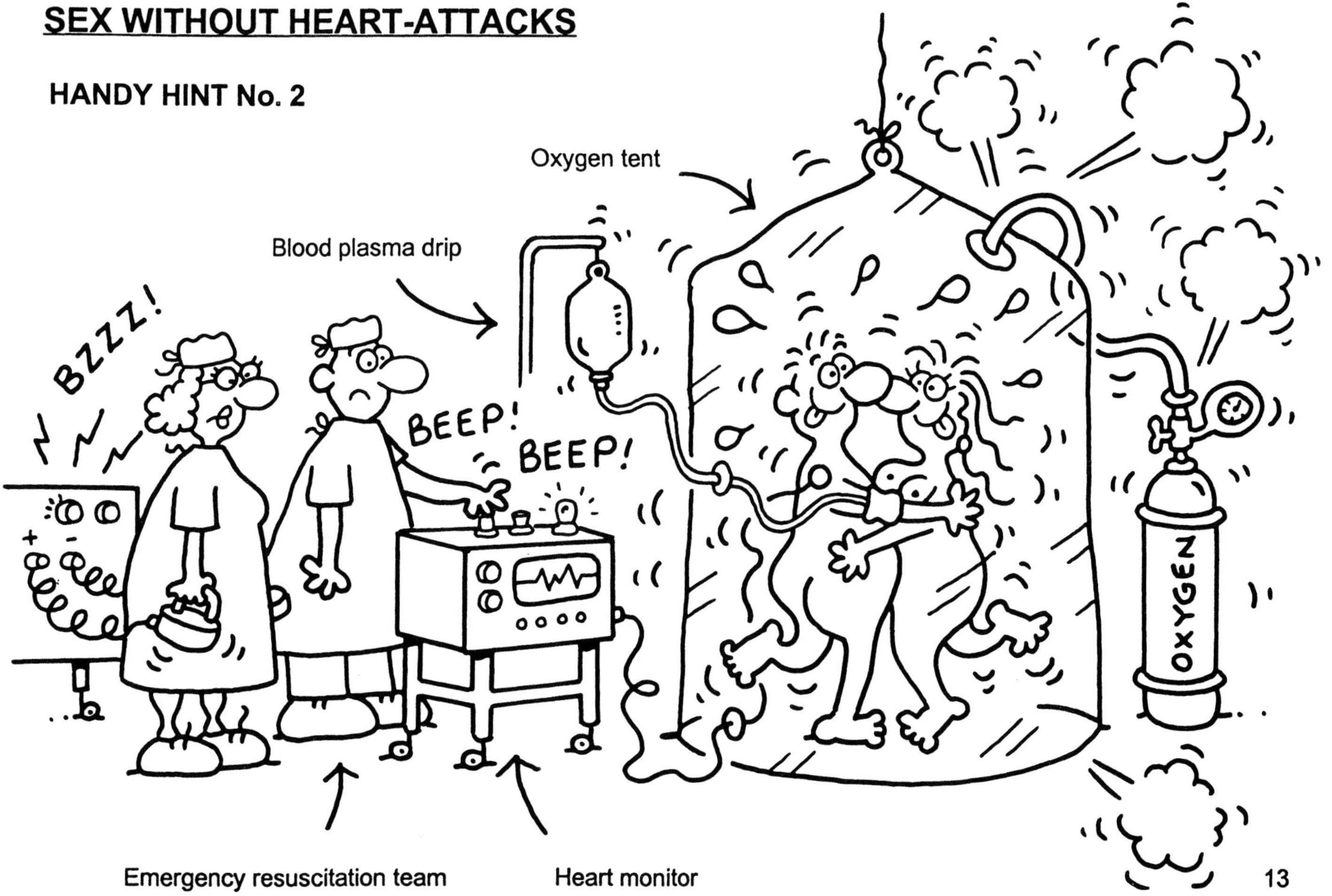
Oxygen tent
Blood plasma drip
BZZZ!
BEEP!
BEEP!
OXYGEN
Emergency resuscitation team
Heart monitor

COPING WITH THE BIRTHDAY PARTY

HANDY HINT No. 1: The birthday nosh-up

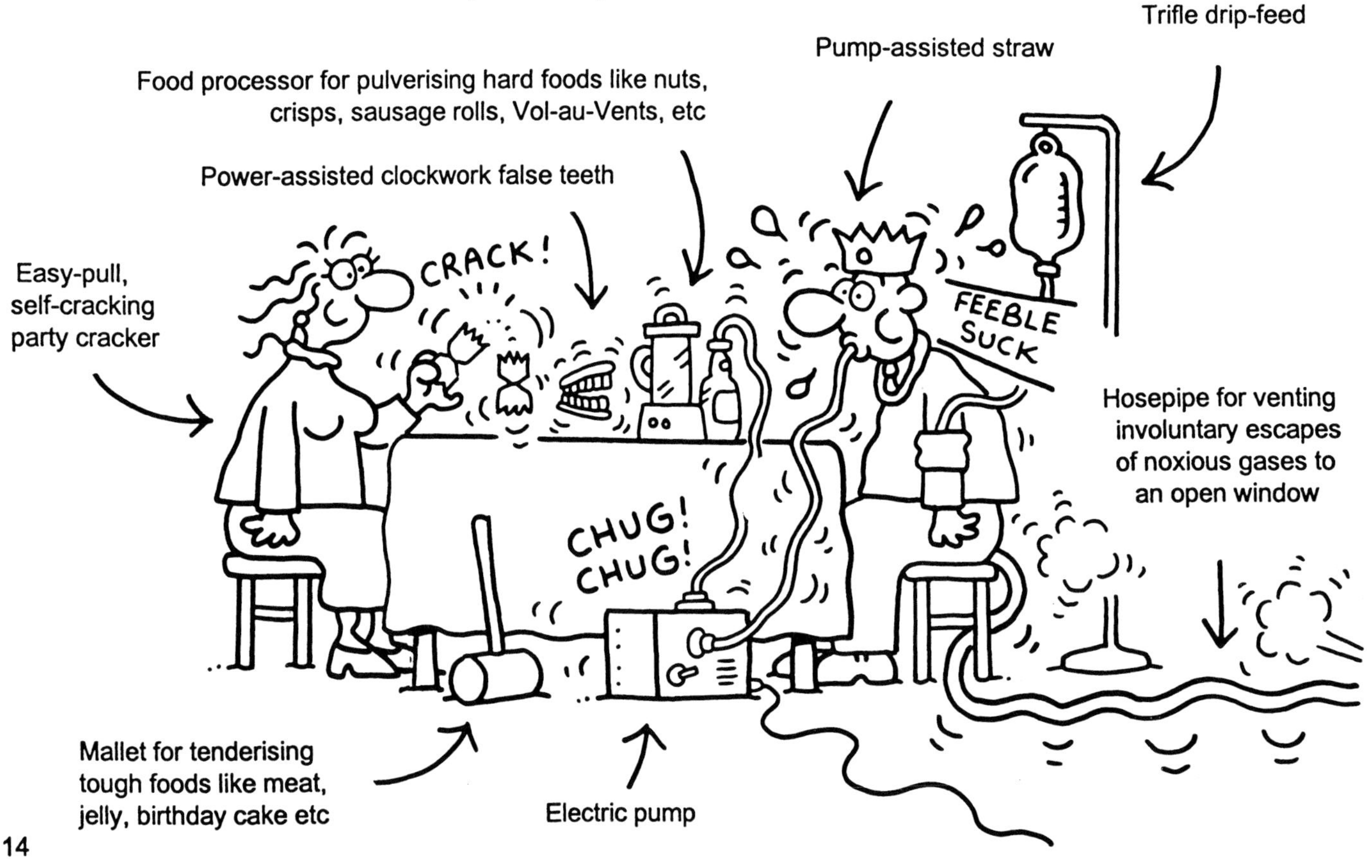
Trifle drip-feed
Pump-assisted straw
Food processor for pulverising hard foods like nuts, crisps, sausage rolls, Vol-au-Vents, etc
Power-assisted clockwork false teeth
Easy-pull, self-cracking party cracker
CRACK!
FEEBLE SUCK
Hosepipe for venting involuntary escapes of noxious gases to an open window
CHUG! CHUG!
Mallet for tenderising tough foods like meat, jelly, birthday cake etc
Electric pump

COPING WITH THE BIRTHDAY BOOZE-UP

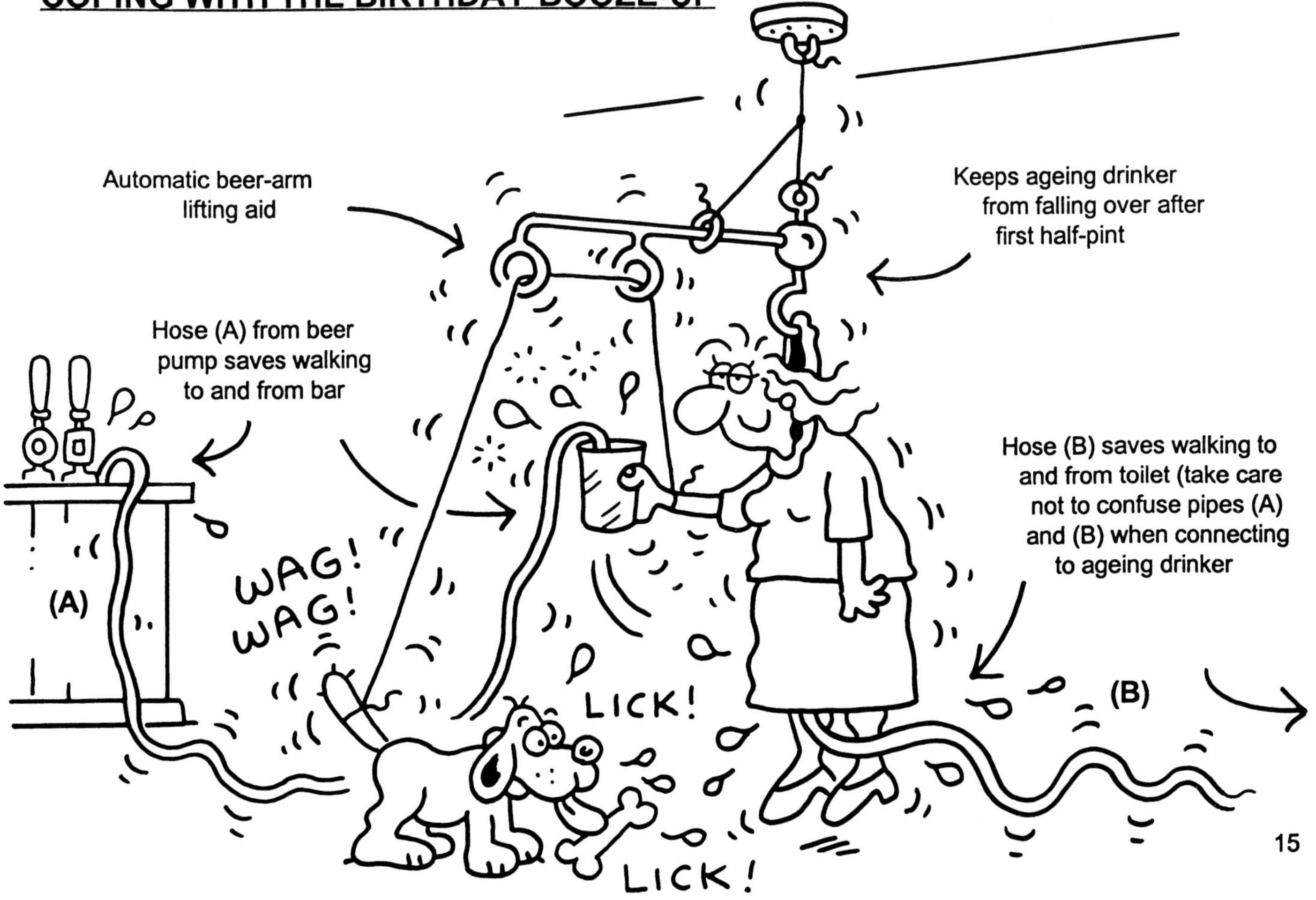
Automatic beer-arm lifting aid
Keeps ageing drinker from falling over after first half-pint
Hose (A) from beer pump saves walking to and from bar
Hose (B) saves walking to and from toilet (take care not to confuse pipes (A) and (B) when connecting to ageing drinker
(A)
(B)
WAG! WAG!
LICK!
LICK!

SURVIVING ON THE DANCE FLOOR

HANDY HINT No. 1: Getting your creaky old bones moving and grooving

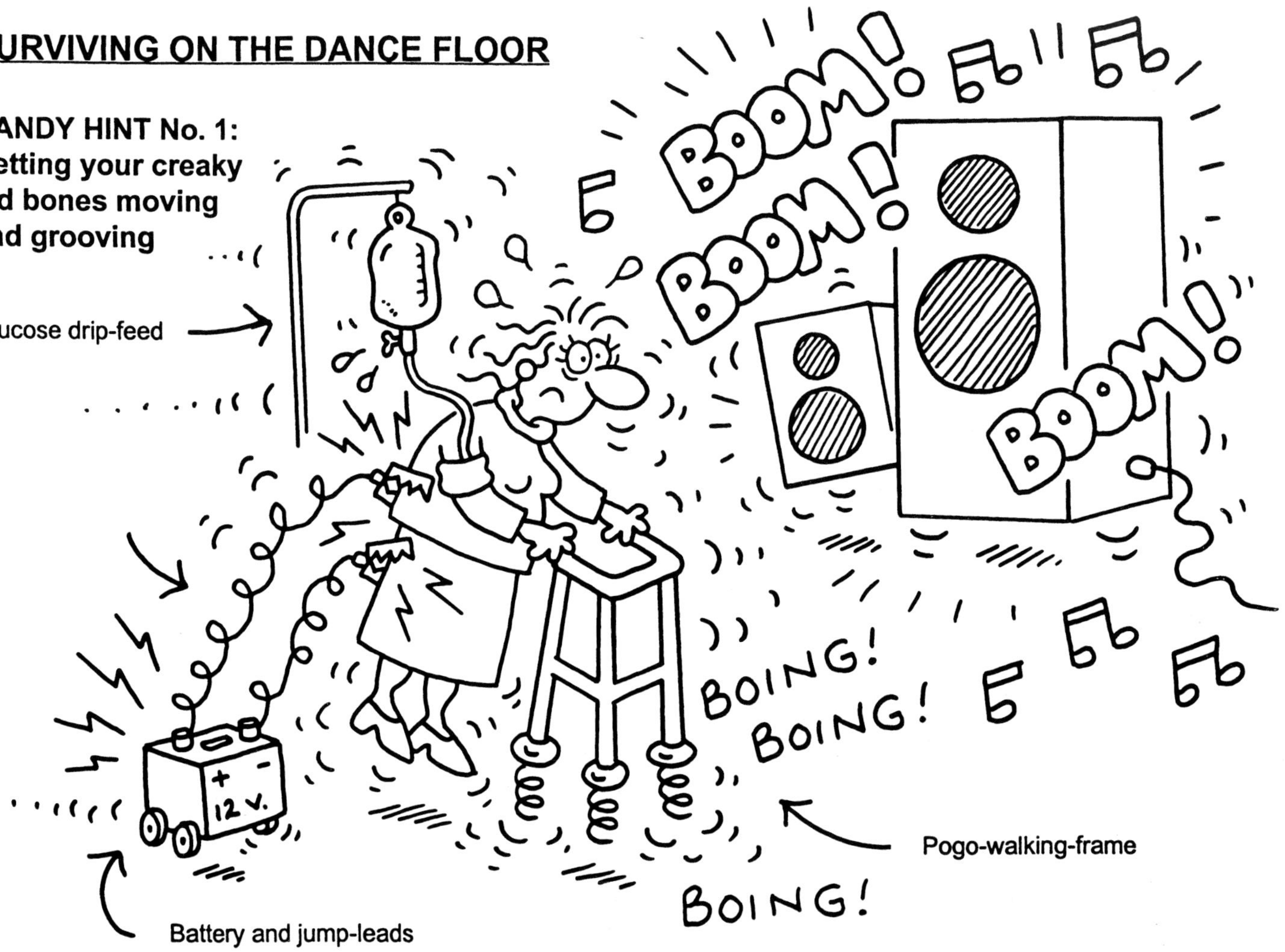
Glucose drip-feed
BOOM!
BOOM!
BOOM!
+ −
12 V.
BOING!
BOING!
BOING!
Pogo-walking-frame
Battery and jump-leads

AVOIDING DROOPY BOOBS

Ultra-uplift helium-filled inflatable push-up bra for extra cleavage-creating, boob-lifting, eye-catching, gravity-defying effect

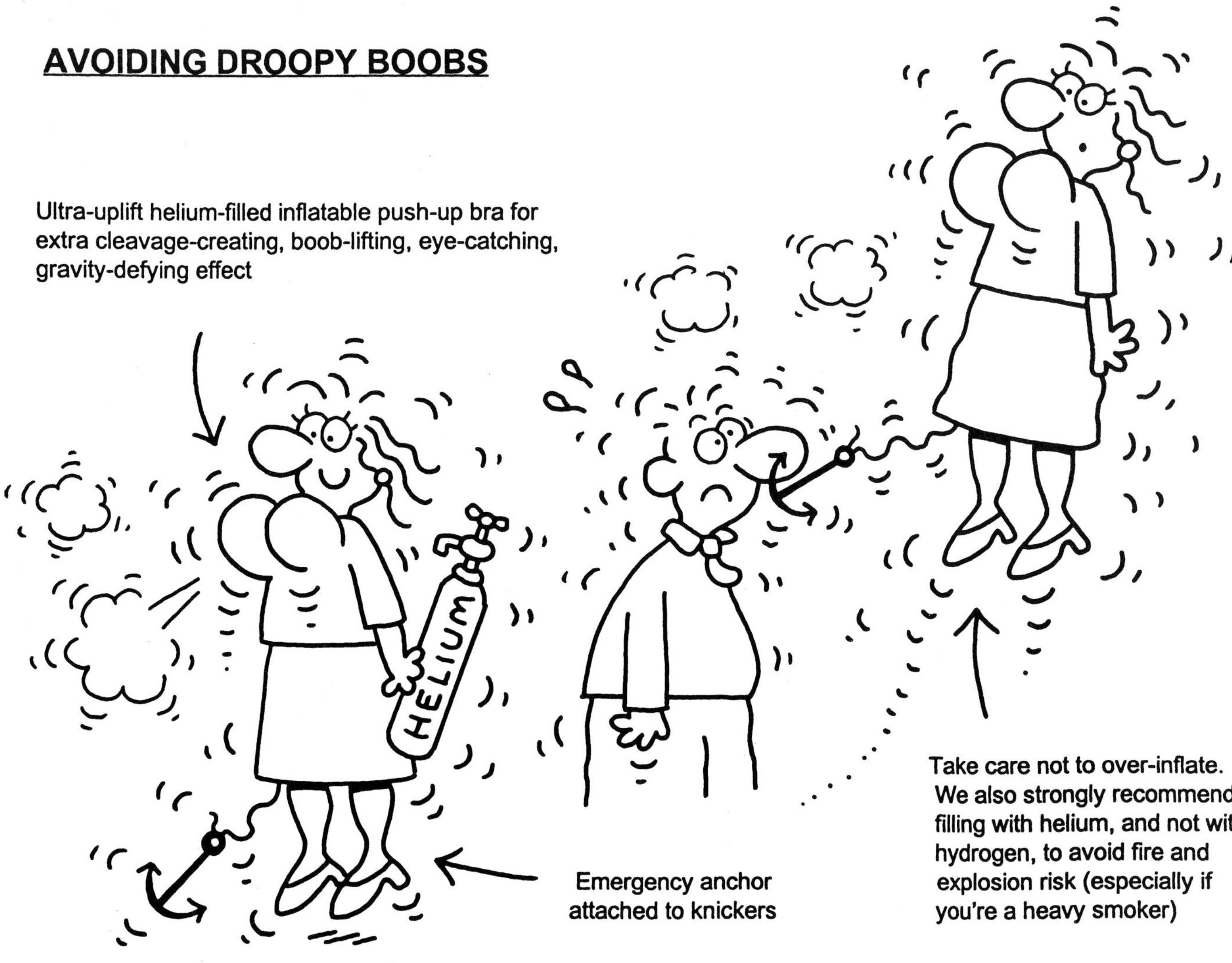
HELIUM

Emergency anchor attached to knickers

Take care not to over-inflate. We also strongly recommend filling with helium, and not with hydrogen, to avoid fire and explosion risk (especially if you're a heavy smoker)

COPING WITH THE BIRTHDAY PARTY

HANDY HINT No. 2: The birthday snogging session

Slobber-proof pad and pen for writing urgent messages to your snogging partner

Life-like rubber tongue extension and support sheath

Check air-tank level at regular intervals

Ideally, choose a snogging partner with experience and/or qualifications in both the kiss-of-life and French-kissing

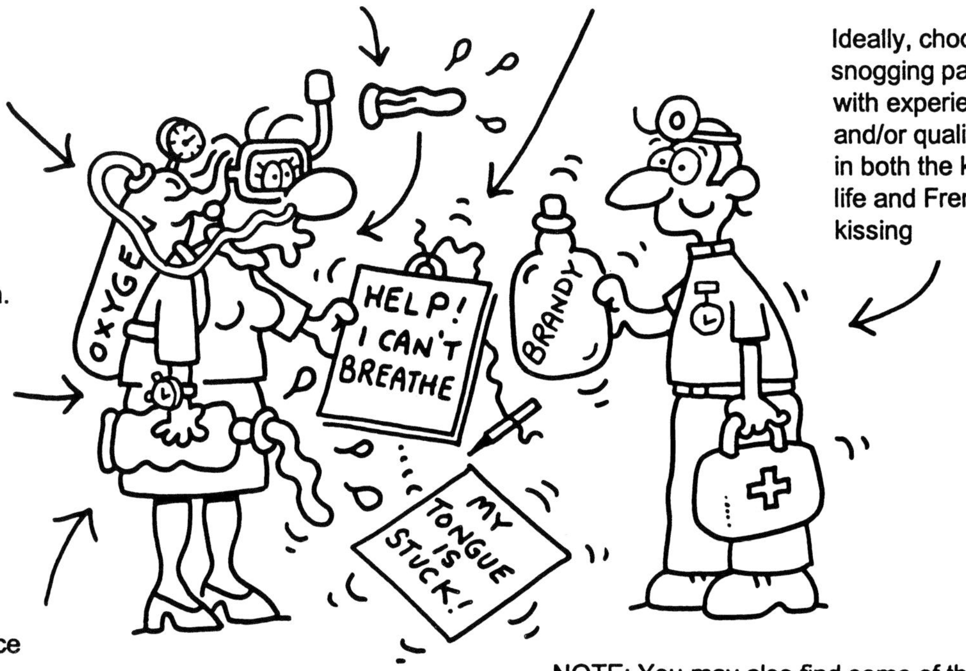

OXYGE
HELP! I CAN'T BREATHE
BRANDY
MY TONGUE IS STUCK!

Drool-proof diver's watch. Take care to avoid long extended periods of snogging submersion and rapid re-surfacing, which can cause an attack of the 'bends'

'Stay-Stiff' lip cream for prolonged endurance and staying power

NOTE: You may also find some of these tips useful during sex in the '69' position

SURVIVING ON THE DANCE FLOOR

HANDY HINT No. 2: Keeping going all night and avoiding injuries

Your rave-drug of choice (we strongly recommend herbal Ginseng with arnica, echinacea and vitamin supplements

Safety net (in case you keel over from exhaustion after just one dance or nod off at your usual bed-time)

The after-party shower

200 LTR. DEEP-HEAT RUB LOTION

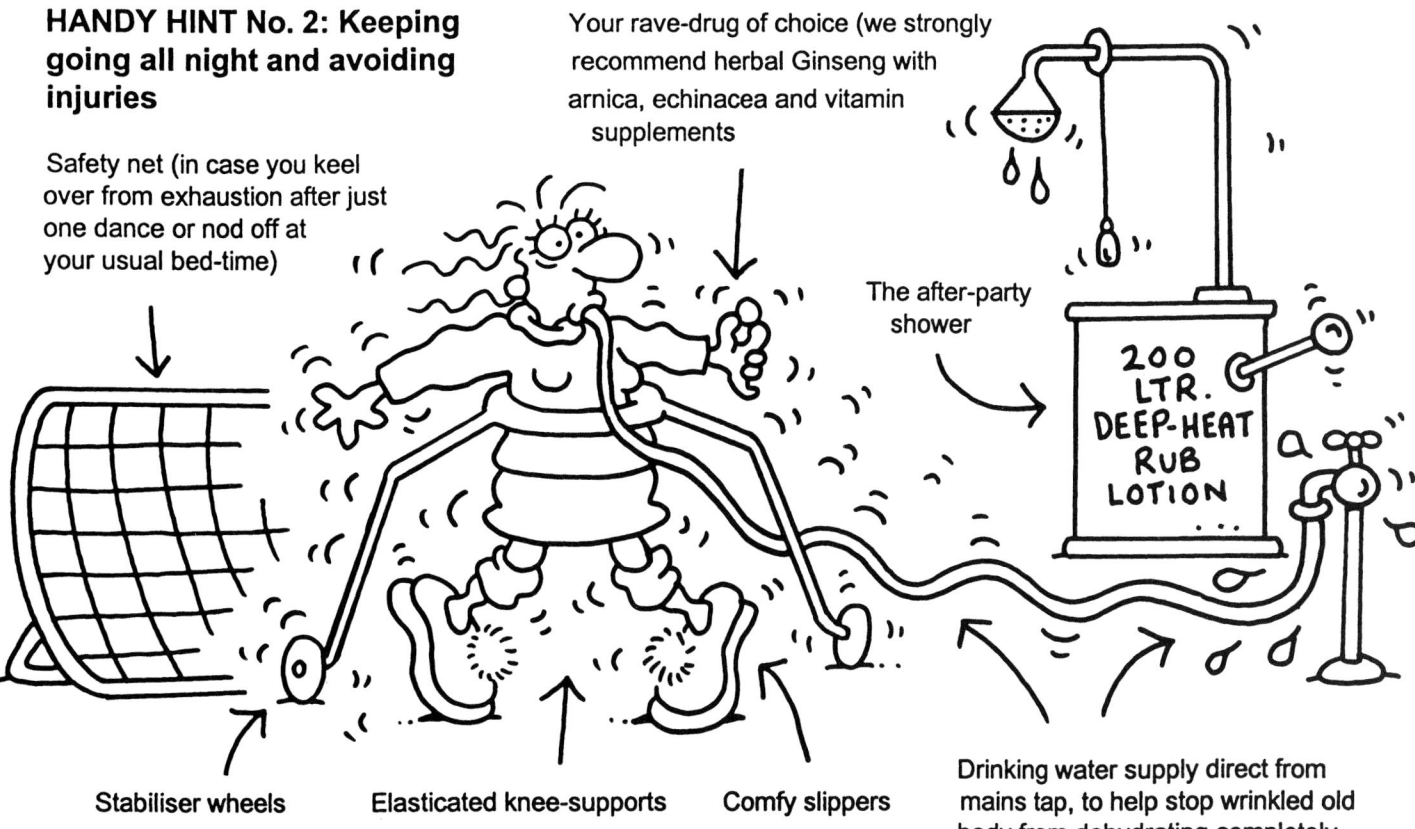

Stabiliser wheels

Elasticated knee-supports

Comfy slippers

Drinking water supply direct from mains tap, to help stop wrinkled old body from dehydrating completely and blowing away like a dead leaf

19

COPING WITH THE BIRTHDAY PARTY

HANDY HINT No. 3: The after-party throw-up

Keep emergency barf-bag handy at all times, in case doddery old legs fail to get you to the toilet in time

Padded headrest fixes to toilet cistern with rubber sucker attachment

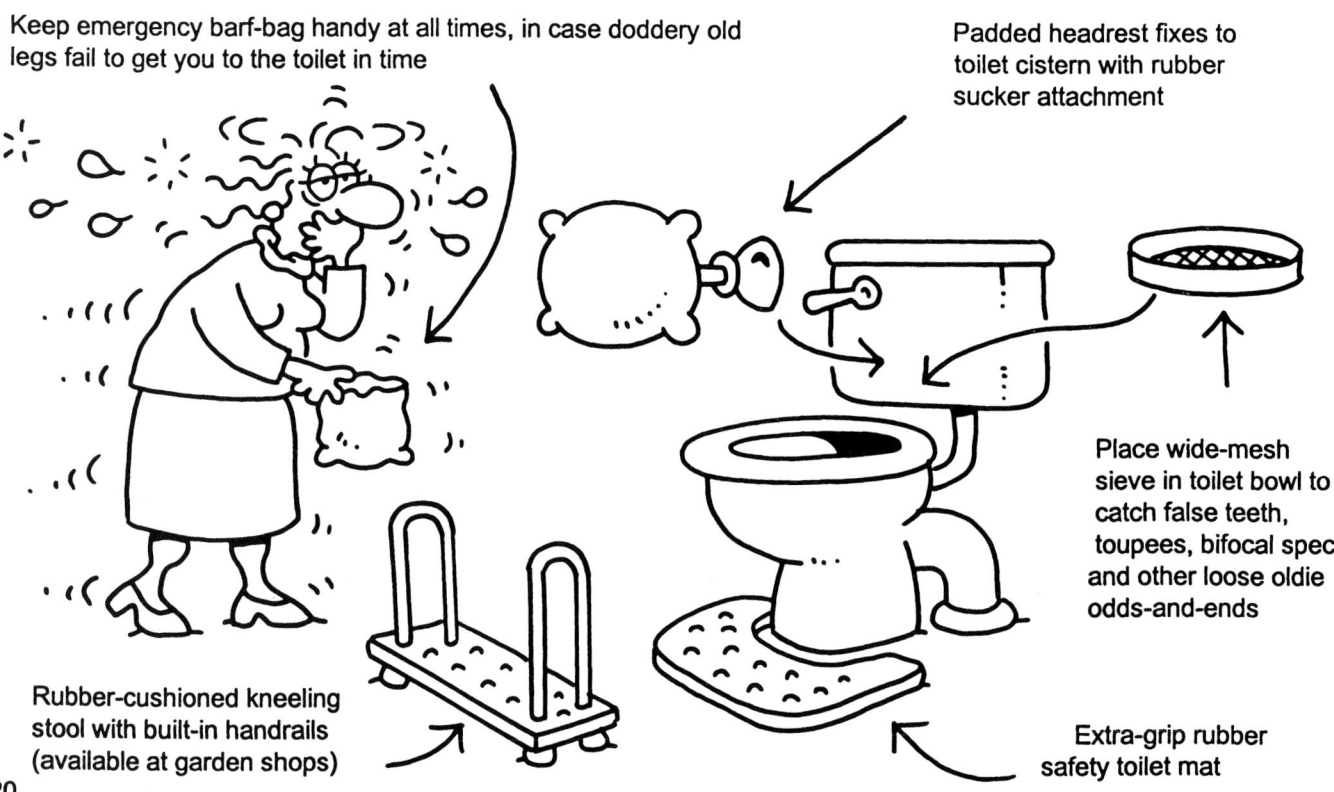

Place wide-mesh sieve in toilet bowl to catch false teeth, toupees, bifocal specs and other loose oldie odds-and-ends

Rubber-cushioned kneeling stool with built-in handrails (available at garden shops)

Extra-grip rubber safety toilet mat

FAKING MULTIPLE-ORGASMS WITHOUT THE EFFORT

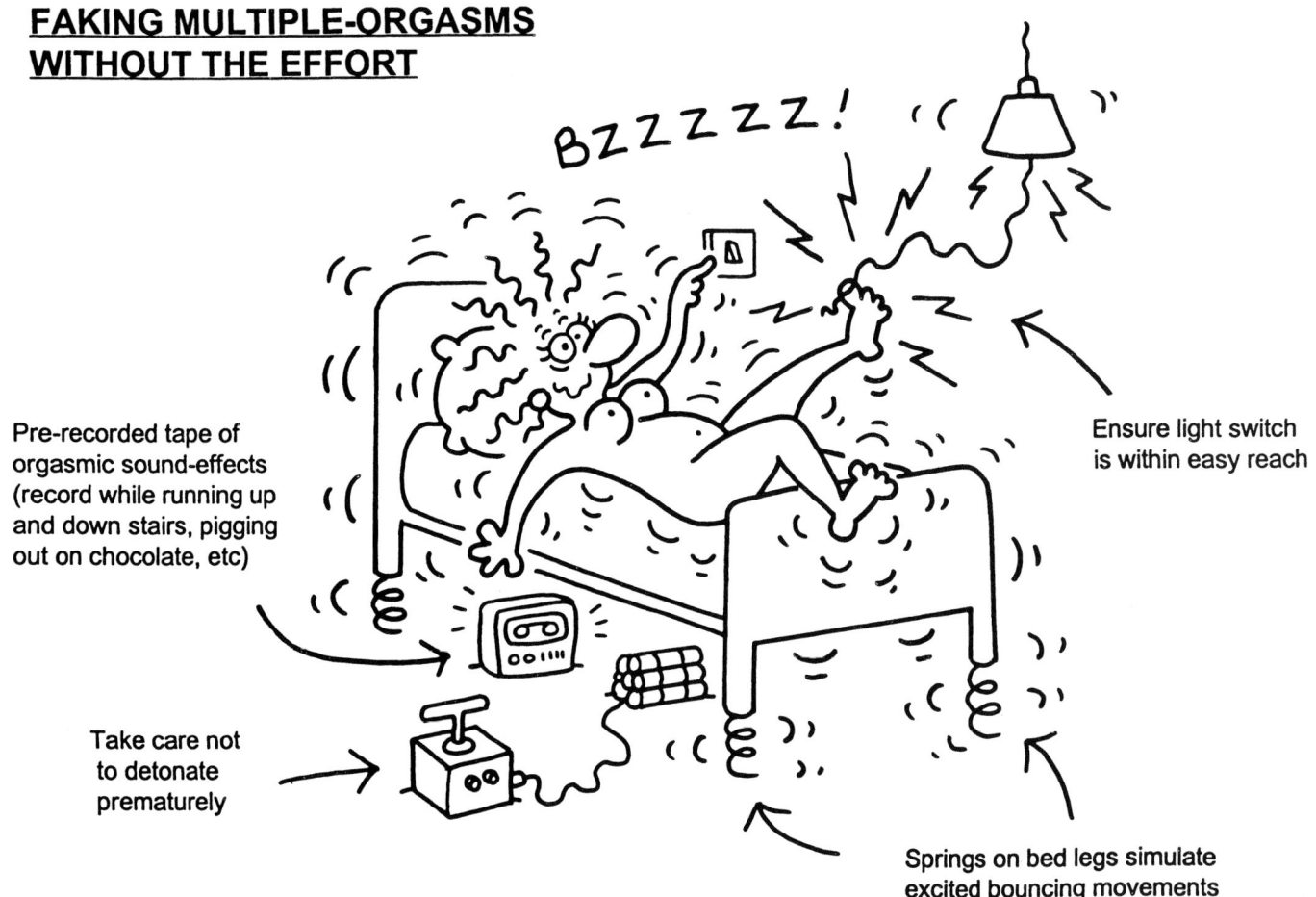

BZZZZZ!

Pre-recorded tape of orgasmic sound-effects (record while running up and down stairs, pigging out on chocolate, etc)

Take care not to detonate prematurely

Ensure light switch is within easy reach

Springs on bed legs simulate excited bouncing movements

BEING A TRENDY OLDIE

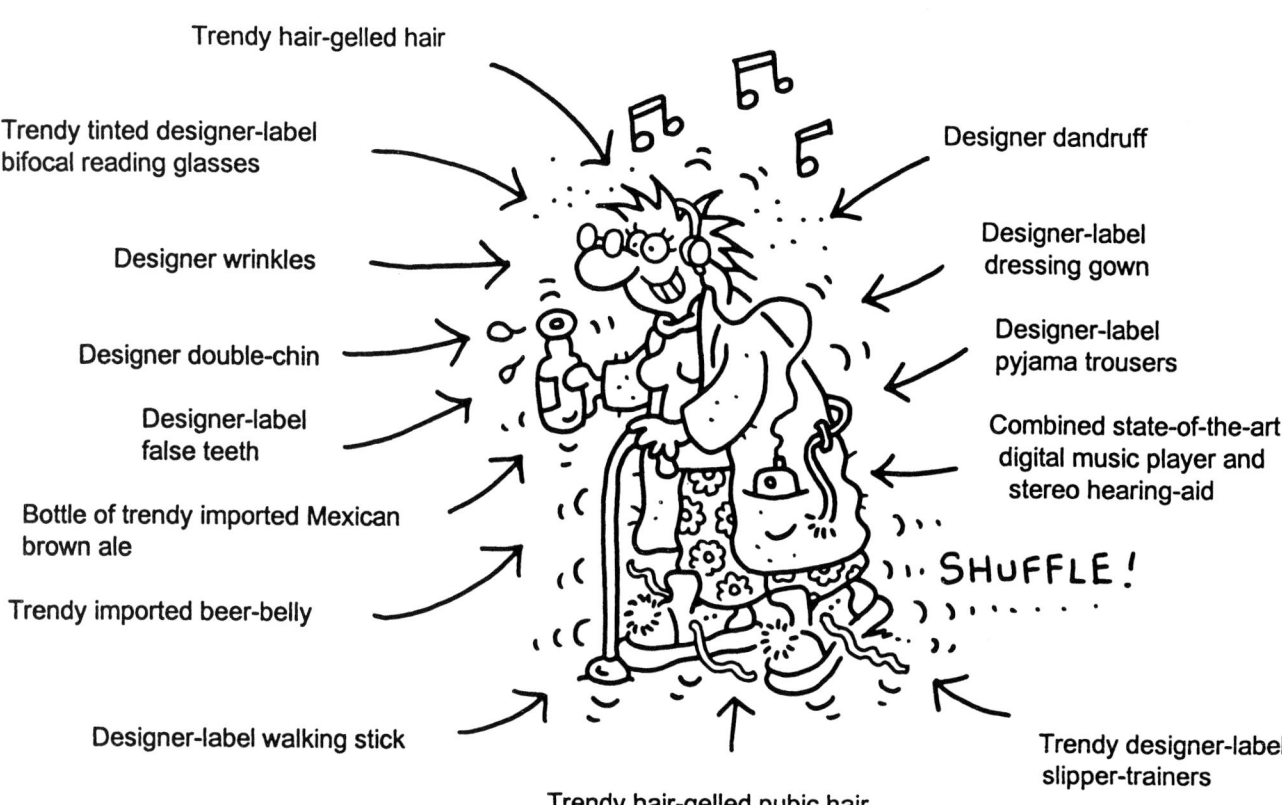

Trendy hair-gelled hair

Trendy tinted designer-label bifocal reading glasses

Designer wrinkles

Designer double-chin

Designer-label false teeth

Bottle of trendy imported Mexican brown ale

Trendy imported beer-belly

Designer-label walking stick

Designer dandruff

Designer-label dressing gown

Designer-label pyjama trousers

Combined state-of-the-art digital music player and stereo hearing-aid

SHUFFLE!

Trendy designer-label slipper-trainers

Trendy hair-gelled pubic hair

HEALTHY- LIVING MADE EASY

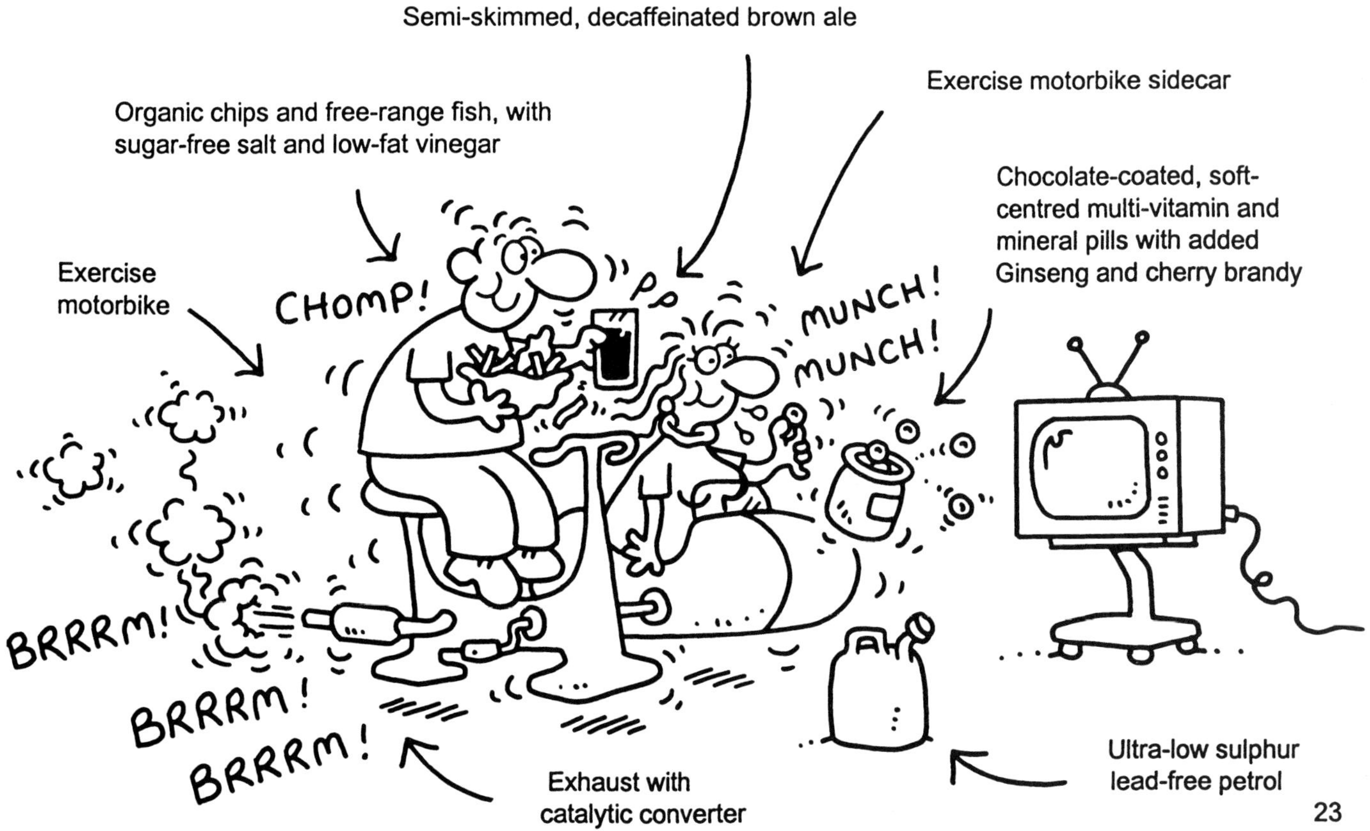
Semi-skimmed, decaffeinated brown ale
Exercise motorbike sidecar
Organic chips and free-range fish, with sugar-free salt and low-fat vinegar
Chocolate-coated, soft-centred multi-vitamin and mineral pills with added Ginseng and cherry brandy
Exercise motorbike
CHOMP!
MUNCH!
MUNCH!
BRRRM!
BRRRM!
BRRRM!
Exhaust with catalytic converter
Ultra-low sulphur lead-free petrol

SEX AIDS FOR OLDIES

HANDY HINT No. 1

Orthopaedic water-bed (fill with raspberry jelly, custard, rice pudding, semolina, yogurt, etc, according to degree of back-supporting firmness required and type of after-sex snack preferred)

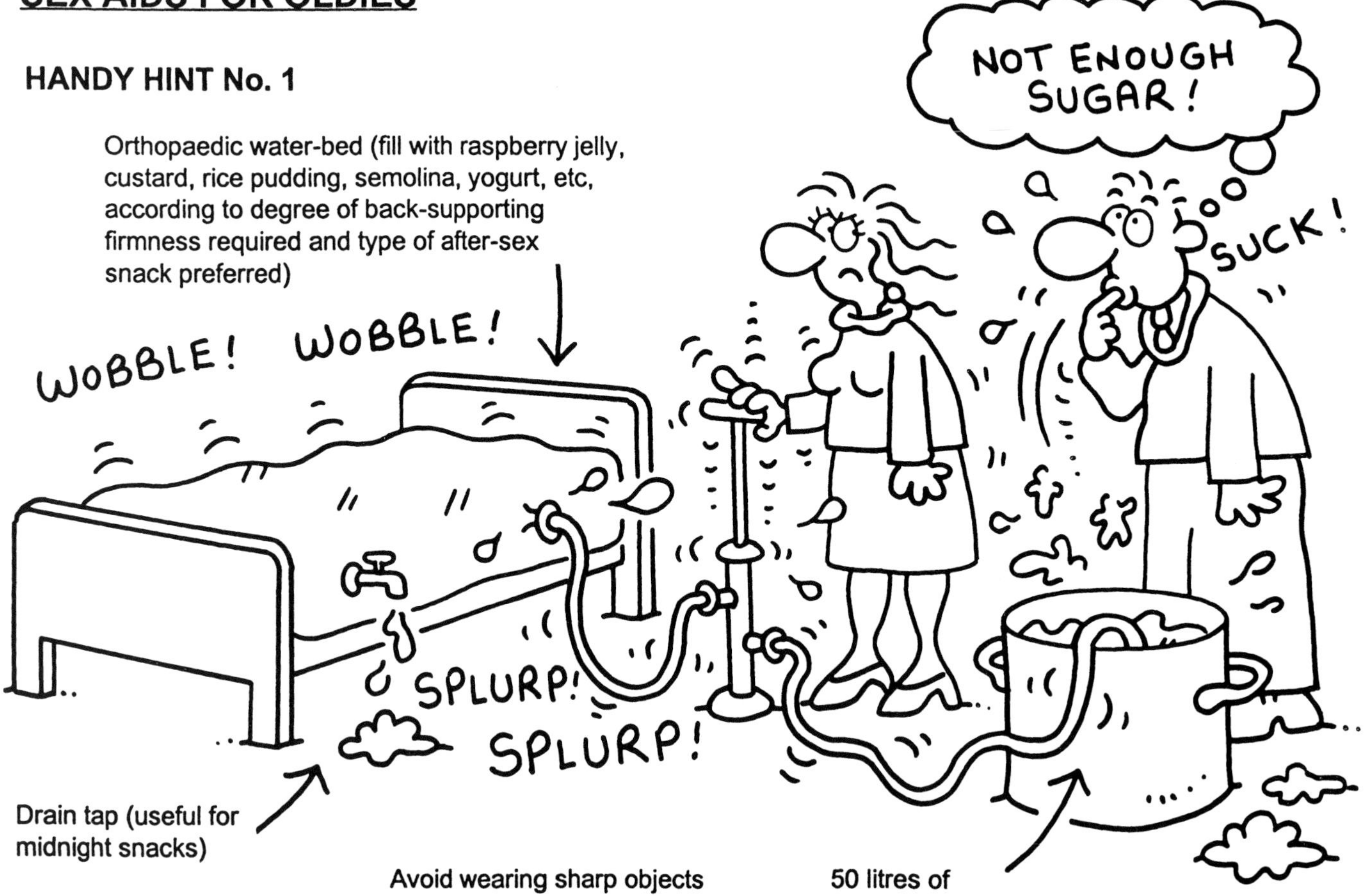

NOT ENOUGH SUGAR!
SUCK!
WOBBLE! WOBBLE!
SPLURP!
SPLURP!

Drain tap (useful for midnight snacks)

Avoid wearing sharp objects (stiletto heels, spurs etc)

50 litres of warm custard

SEX AIDS FOR OLDIES

HANDY HINT No. 2

Lifelike "Oldie" vibrator

Complete with flat batteries for realistic oldie male-type performance (guaranteed to last three minutes maximum)

Scientifically moulded "droopy" shape for minimum stimulation and sensation (you'll never know it's there, so will not Interfere with normal activities, such as watching TV, clipping toe-nails, shaving legs, etc)

Does not incorporate any perceptible up-and-down motion or wiggle, swivel, or any other at all exciting/interesting movements

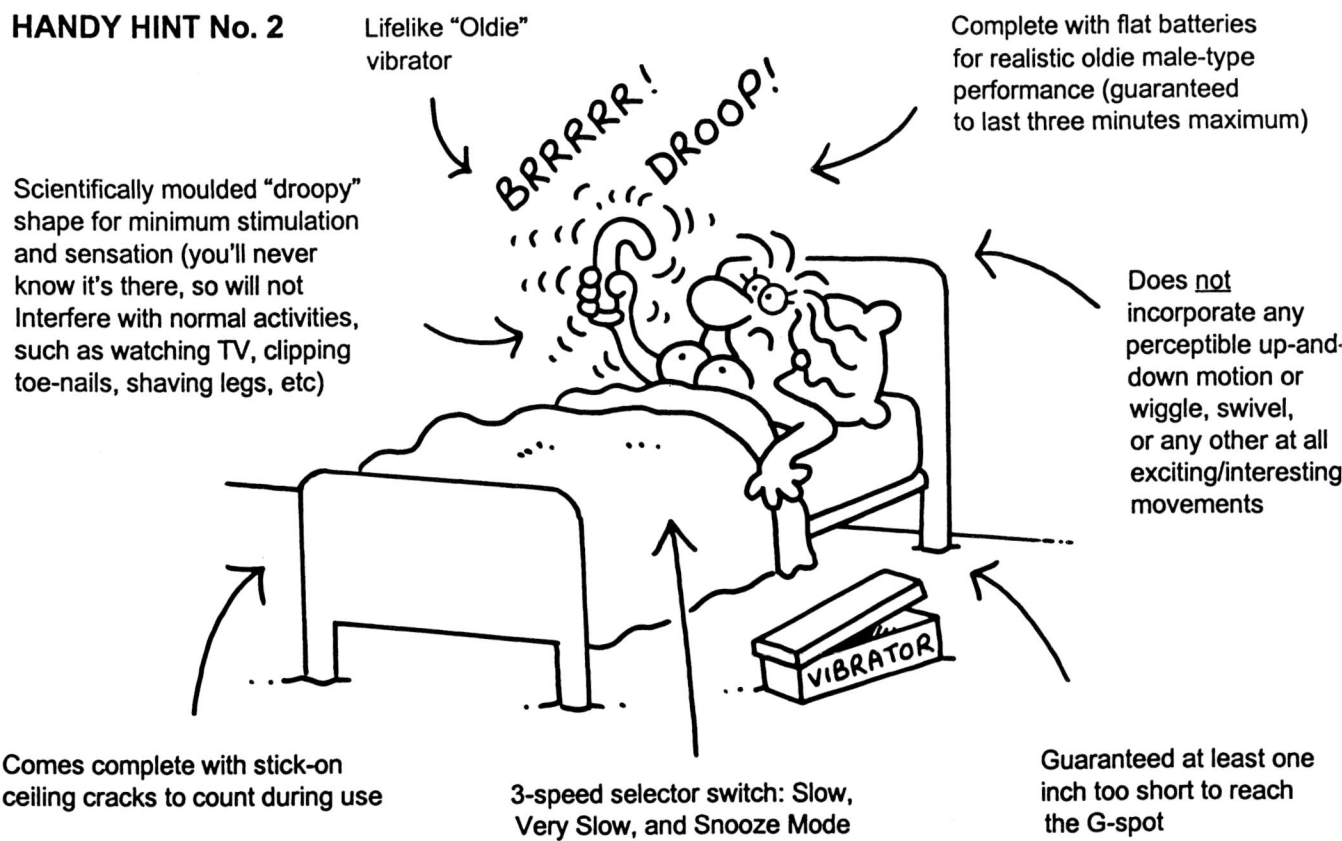

Comes complete with stick-on ceiling cracks to count during use

3-speed selector switch: Slow, Very Slow, and Snooze Mode

Guaranteed at least one inch too short to reach the G-spot

SEX AIDS FOR OLDIES

HANDY HINT No. 3

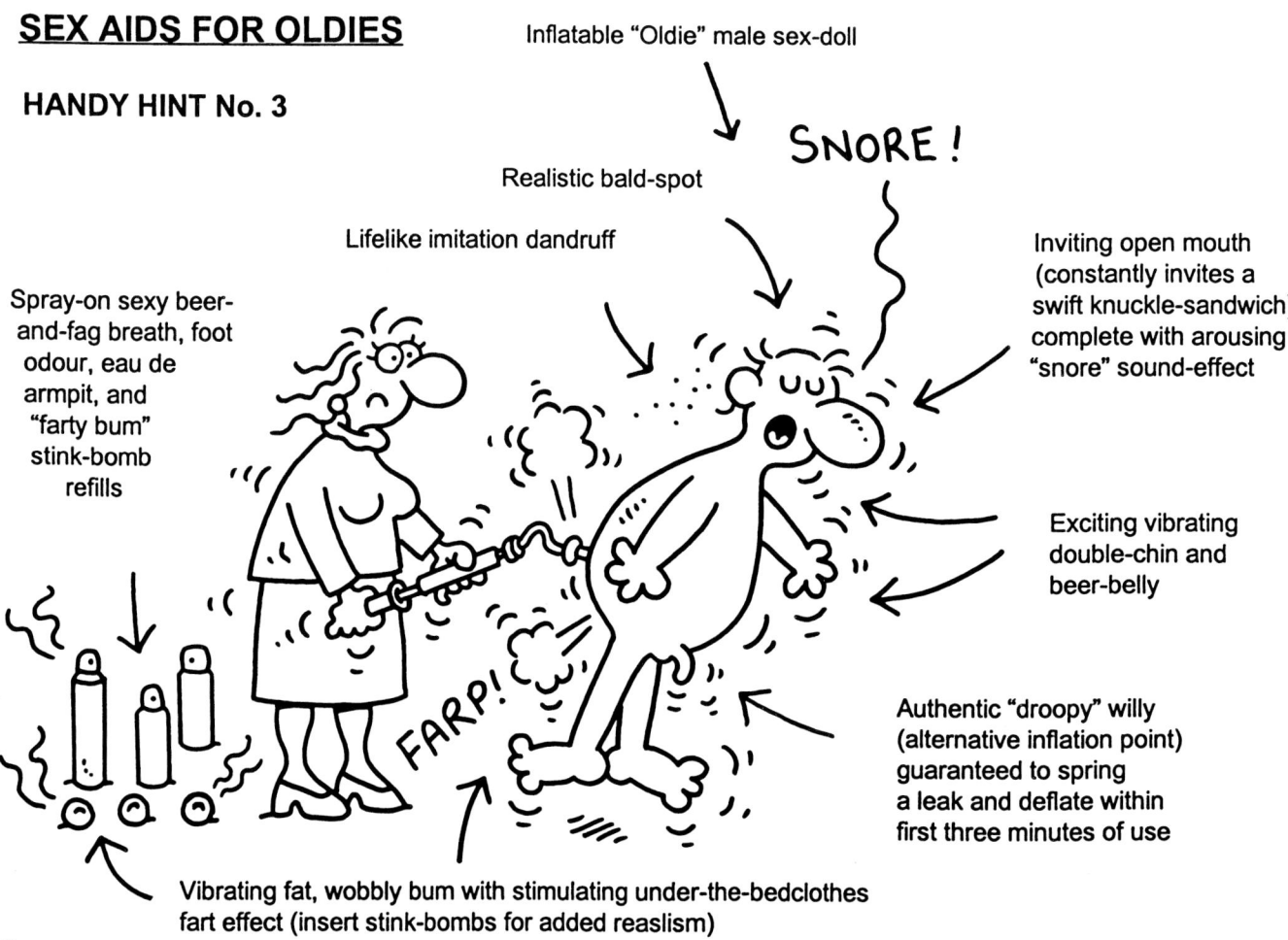

Inflatable "Oldie" male sex-doll

SNORE !

Realistic bald-spot

Lifelike imitation dandruff

Inviting open mouth (constantly invites a swift knuckle-sandwich) complete with arousing "snore" sound-effect

Spray-on sexy beer-and-fag breath, foot odour, eau de armpit, and "farty bum" stink-bomb refills

Exciting vibrating double-chin and beer-belly

FARP!

Authentic "droopy" willy (alternative inflation point) guaranteed to spring a leak and deflate within first three minutes of use

Vibrating fat, wobbly bum with stimulating under-the-bedclothes fart effect (insert stink-bombs for added reaslism)

AN OLDIES' GUIDE TO EROGENOUS ZONES

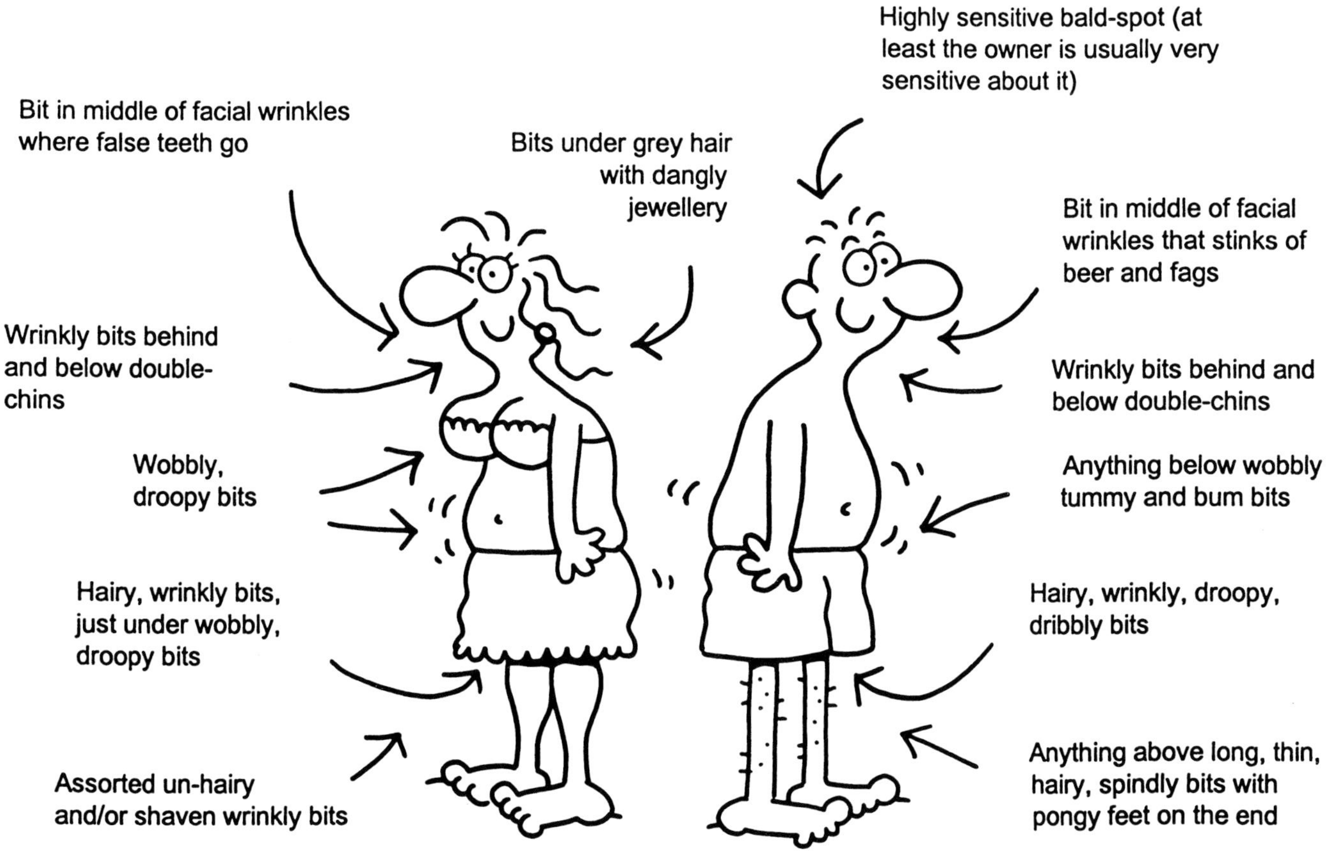

Highly sensitive bald-spot (at least the owner is usually very sensitive about it)
Bit in middle of facial wrinkles where false teeth go
Bits under grey hair with dangly jewellery
Bit in middle of facial wrinkles that stinks of beer and fags
Wrinkly bits behind and below double-chins
Wrinkly bits behind and below double-chins
Wobbly, droopy bits
Anything below wobbly tummy and bum bits
Hairy, wrinkly bits, just under wobbly, droopy bits
Hairy, wrinkly, droopy, dribbly bits
Assorted un-hairy and/or shaven wrinkly bits
Anything above long, thin, hairy, spindly bits with pongy feet on the end

FOREPLAY FOR OLDIES

1) Do washing-up and/or put kids to bed

2) Work out mortgage payments and/or try to balance cheque book and plan monthly budget

3) Have a good cry

4) Collapse in front of television

5) Nip down to pub for a quick pint (usually one partner only)

6) Eat take-away, watch late film, fall asleep on settee

7) Make Horlicks/cocoa/drinking-chocolate. Try to balance cheque book, plan monthly budget, etc

8) 11 p.m. partner No. 1 cleans teeth and goes to bed

9) 1 a.m. partner No. 2 turns off TV, cleans teeth and goes to bed

10) 1.05 a.m. partner No. 1 gets up to see to kids/ have a pee/try to balance cheque book/work out monthly budget/have a good cry/drink bottle of gin

11) Have sex (in the unlikely event that you should actually reach the stage of having sex, see the advice on the following pages)

SNORE !

NOOKIES FOR OLDIES (A REFRESHER COURSE)

1) Visit doctor for thorough pre-sex fitness check-up (blood-pressure, potential heart problems, possible shortness of breath, halitosis, smelly feet, etc)

2) Pre-sex fitness training programme: Minimum 3 weeks jogging, exercise bike, weight-lifting, press-ups, tongue-building and sucking exercises

3) Check correct and safe functioning of all basic equipment and any surgical, kinky or electrical appliances (including battery charges) especially if any of your equipment and/or appliances have not been used for some time.

   Ensure that any mains-powered electrical appliances are fitted with circuit-breakers for added safety during use in moist, dribbly operating conditions

4) Foreplay: (see also previous page) Note: evening-class refresher courses in basic foreplay techniques may be available at some more progressive local colleges

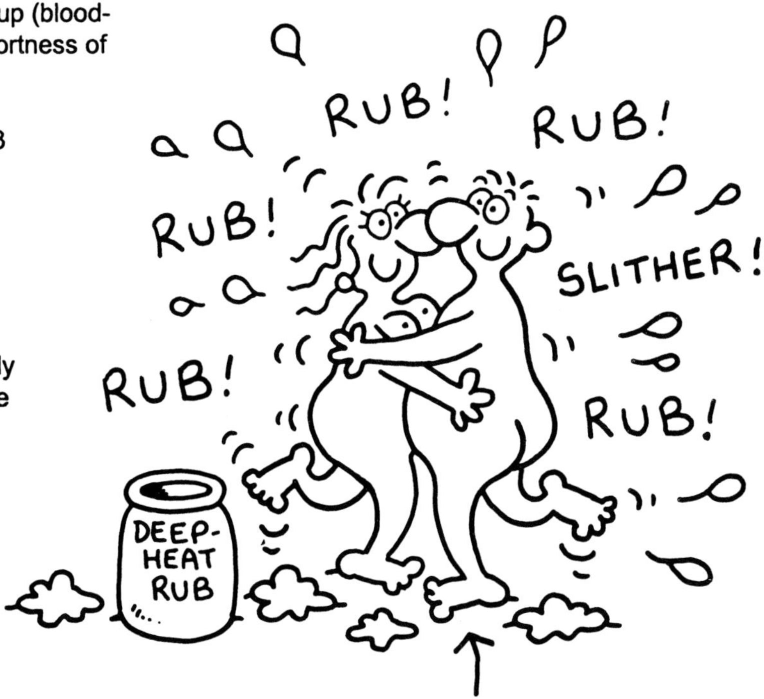
RUB!
RUB!
RUB!
SLITHER!
RUB!
RUB!
DEEP-
HEAT
RUB

A sensual massage with deep-heat rub can prove a stimulating and erotic experience, while at the same time soothing aching aged muscles

5) Check that you have partner. Check that partner is awake/breathing/inflated

6) Commence having sex (it's like riding a bicycle - no matter how long it's been, you'll remember how to do it, but do expect to fall off once or twice until you get the hang of it again)

7) Wheeze, cough, gasp, stop to catch your breath and wait for the room to stop spinning round

8) Complain about back-ache and stop for a sensual mutual massage with deep-heat rub

9) Break for a cup of tea and/or a read of that that bedside book you've been meaning to finish for ages

10) Repeat steps 5) to 9) until one or other partner starts snoring

11) Recovery and recuperation: Pre-book time off work for post-sex period, appointments with osteopath, chiropractor and orthopaedic surgeon, and fortnight's residential care in rest-home

Note: Timing is vital. Ideally, try to time it so that both partners nod off simultaneously

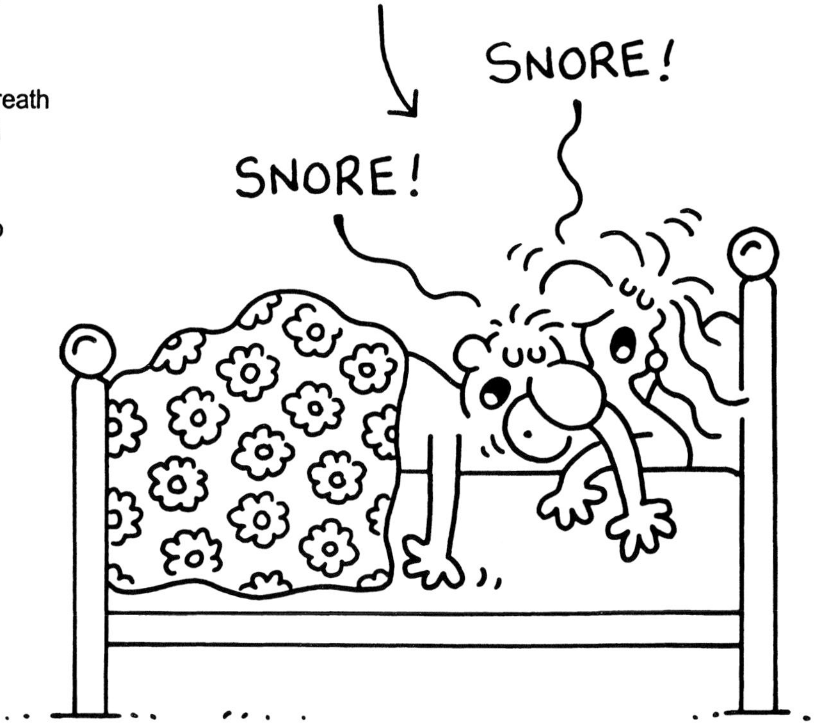
SNORE!
SNORE!

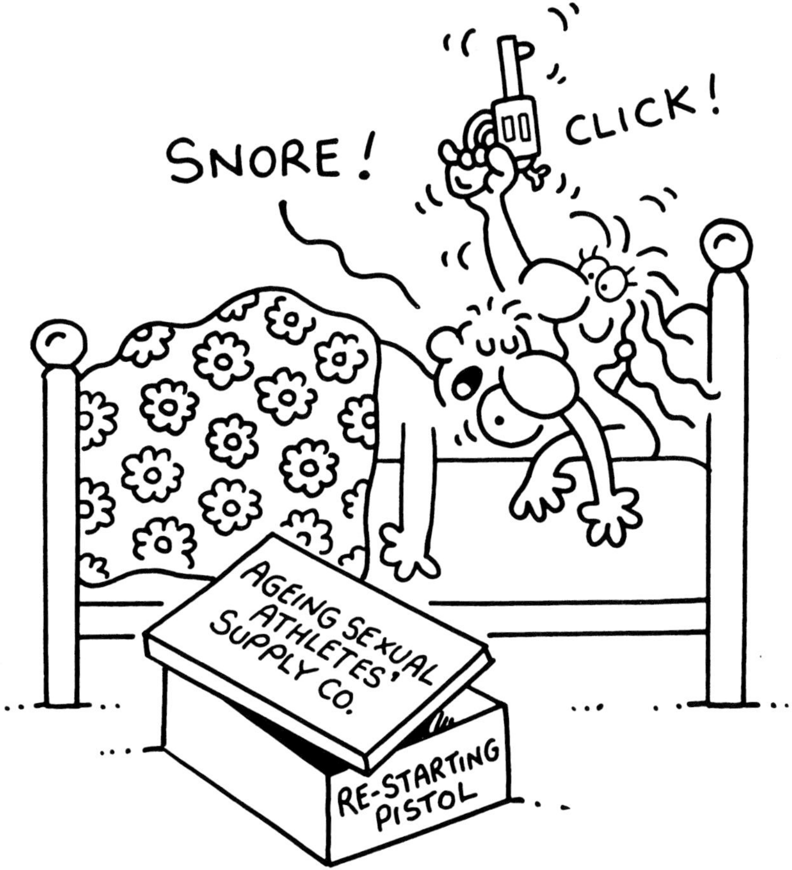
SNORE!
CLICK!
AGEING SEXUAL ATHLETES' SUPPLY CO.
RE-STARTING PISTOL

OTHER BOOKS BY MARTIN BAXENDALE

'THE SNOWDROP GARDEN' - Martin's first novel is a wickedly funny and heart-warming tale of love, misunderstandings and a last-ditch attempt to save one of England's most beautiful woodland snowdrop gardens from the builders' bulldozers. A really great, laugh-out-loud read.

'WHEN WILL MY BABY BRAIN FALL OUT?' - Martin's first children's book. Seven-year-old Millie struggles with her maths homework but then she gets hold of the idea that things will be better when her 'baby brain' falls out, just like a baby tooth, and her cleverer big-girl brain grows in its place. Should Mum and Dad put her straight or play along? A very funny yet charming story that will have children laughing out loud.

And some of Martin's best-selling cartoon gift-books:

'Your New Baby, An Owner's Manual' (over 500,000 copies sold).
'How To Be A Baby, An Instruction Manual For Newborns'
'Your Marriage, An Owner's Manual'
'How To Be Married, An Instruction Manual For Newlyweds'
Life After 30, A Survival Guide For Women
'Life After 40, A Survival Guide For Women'
'Life After 40, A Survival Guide For Men'
'Life After 50, A Survival Guide For Women'
'Life After 50, A Survival Guide For Men'
'How To Stay Awake During Sex (and other handy hints on coping with old age)'
'Martin Baxendale's Better Sex Guide'
'The Relationship Survival Guide'
'A Very Rude Book About Willies'
'The Cat Owner's Survival Guide'
'The Dog Owner's Survival Guide'
'Your Man, An Owner's Manual'
'Calm Down!! The Stress Survival Guide'
'Your Pregnancy, A Survival Guide'
'Women Are Wonderful, Men Are A Mess'
The Garden Owner's Survival Guide
The Facebook Addict's Survival Guide

These and other books by Martin Baxendale can be ordered from www.amazon.co.uk (search for Martin Baxendale, or search by title, in 'books') and from other online bookstores or any High Street bookshop.